Acts of MAGICAL Resistance

Phil Hine

Twisted Trunk 2023

Published in 2023 by Twisted Trunk

BM Twisted Trunk, London WC1N 3XX

phil@twistedtrunkbooks.com

https://enfolding.org/books/

ISBN: 978-1-9162366-6-0

Acknowledgements

With thanks to: Lawrence Burton, Al Cummins, Adrian Harris, Layla and Phil Legard, Patricia MacCormack, Christina Oakley Harrington, David Southwell and Maria Strutz.

Cover Photo by Maria Strutz.

Unless specified otherwise, all images are from my personal collection..

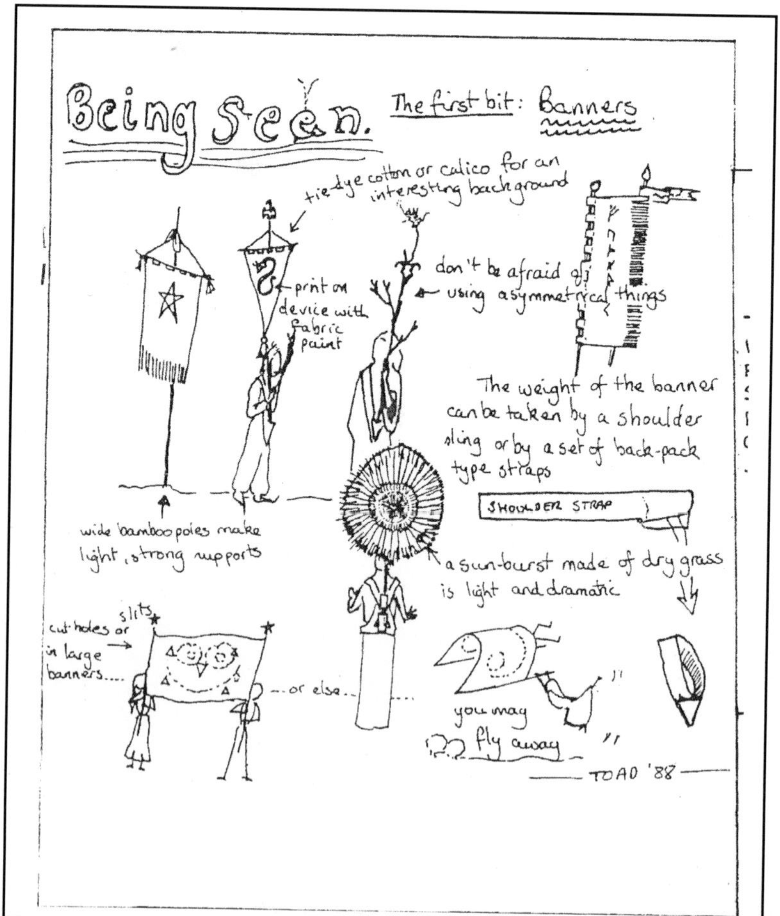

A visual guide to making Banners, from *Moonshine* #13, 1988.

Contents

If magic is "the art of causing change in accordance with will", then political acts, acts of protest and resistance, acts that speak truth to power, that push for change, are acts of magic.

Starhawk, *Dreaming the Dark*

Introduction

In February 2023, Patricia MacCormack and myself jointly held a presentation at Helgi's Bar, London, entitled Queer(y)ing Chaos Magick. My contribution to the event was, for the most part, a romp through different approaches to magical political activisms that I'd participated in over the course of the last 40-odd years. This small book was inspired by that event.

Acts of Magical Resistance is a collection of reflections, accounts and historical snippets about magical activism—the use of magic as a mode of political resistance. I am focusing, for the most part most on the United Kingdom, with the odd nod in the direction of India or North America. Why focus on the UK? There has been a good deal of excellent writing over the last decade on the practicalities of magical activism in North America and the histories of movements such as the Women's International Terrorist Conspiracy from Hell (W.I.T.C.H.), but it seems to me that magical activism in the UK has not received much attention. This isn't surprising. Much of it took place before the internet became the repository of collective memory, and was circulated, for the most part, through the UK's vibrant alternative print culture of zines and flyers.

Similarly, many former activists are loath to discuss their activities. It is enough for many of them that they've done what they did, and they don't feel a need to seek recognition for their efforts, or to boast about their results on social media. Again, this is understandable.

Why then, this book? I feel it is useful for contemporary practitioners involved in magical activism to know what previous generations have attempted, and some of the methods they chose to go about it. Those methods might not be deemed applicable to the contemporary situation—either ethically or practically. But at a time when peaceful protesters are increasingly subject to being arrested; when protest against climate change is being labelled as a form of terrorism; when wearing a t-shirt can be a cause for arrest in the UK, or drag performance in the U.S., perhaps it is useful to know what magical approaches have been tried in the past.

Using magical means to resist oppression can be a contentious subject. There are voices still raised in magical communities arguing that magic and politics should not mix. Needless to say, I have always disagreed with this view.

Some years ago, I learnt a powerful lesson in sorcery by watching an adept of the art at work. I was visiting the High Priestess of a local witch coven. Whilst idly glancing through the evening paper, she came across a report of a rapist prowling in the district. She shot up out of the chair, shut up everyone else in the room with an icy glance, and, on reaching the dining table, cleared a space on it by simply sweeping everything onto the floor with a mighty crash. She placed an artist's impression of the rapist from the paper in the centre of the table, grabbed a sausage from the fridge, and, after furiously rummaging in her sewing box, proceeded to methodically drive needles into the sausage, muttering furiously under her breath. The atmosphere in the room was electric. After some minutes, she stalked out of the room and took the sausage into the back garden. On her return, she smiled brightly at the cowering men in the room, and announced 'I think a cup of tea would be nice, don't you?' She offered no explanation or justification for her actions, and never alluded to it afterwards. A week later, the rapist was caught, and later sentenced and incarcerated.

It was only years later that I began to appreciate the power of this woman. She didn't dither around, nor did she worry about ethics, morality, or whether she had the right to act in this way. Nor did she bother with any of the elaborate procedures of ritual magic. By her glance, and her violent clearing of the table, she created a charged atmosphere that rivalled anything I had then experienced in more formal magical surroundings.

This approach I call the magic of need. It arises from circumstance. I recall a neighbour knocking at my door in the early hours of a morning. His car had been stolen. He didn't want the perpetrator to be cursed. He just wanted me to help find his car. I hadn't any experience of doing this, nor did any of the books in my then small occult library have anything to say about recovering stolen cars. But I managed to pull something together (I no longer recall exactly what) and the upshot was that the car was quickly located. Doing the magic of need shows you just what you are capable of when necessity looms before you. Necessity is also very useful in forcing back your personal boundaries—both in terms of what you think you know, what you can do, and, perhaps equally importantly, the limitations that we acquire through reading occult books concerning how magic should—and should not be used.

I generally found that it wasn't unusual for practitioners to carry out magical acts on behalf of their communities, yet at the same there seemed to be very little actual engagement with those communities. It seemed to me that the pagan and occult subculture within the UK in the late 70s and early 80s tended to hold itself aloof from wider society. Again, this began to change as the decade progressed, and esoteric practitioners began to appreciate the benefits of inclusivity and of making their beliefs understandable to wider society. This was a time when being exposed in the newspapers as a witch could get you ostracized at the very least, not to mention bricks through your front room window! The reasons for this change in attitude are complex.

The conservatism of the previous generation of occultists was being challenged through the growing popularity of chaos magic. The repressive policies of the Thatcher government, the growing awareness of looming ecological disaster, and opposition to the presence of American nuclear weapons on British soil had spawned a new generation of Pagans and Occult practitioners who did not view politics as antithetical to the occult. Occult ideas, concepts and imagery seeped into other forms of counter-cultural expression and into the mainstream media; in comics, films, and television, continuing a trend that had begun in the seventies.

Then along came the Satanic Panic (1988-92). It is hard now for people who do not remember that period to grasp how widespread in the media the Panic became. It wasn't just in the tabloids, but in the broadsheets and regional papers too, on radio and television. All it seemed to take was the smallest hint of occult activity in any locality of the country for journalists to pen increasingly alarming purple prose about the dangers of the occult sweeping the country or the threat posed by the growing acceptance of astrology or Halloween festivities. The responses from within the UK's pagan and occult community were varied, but it did give rise to a new generation of representative who could work the media to challenge misconceptions and lies and, more importantly explain to the general public and media esoteric beliefs and attitudes clearly and concisely. That, as much as anything, in my opinion, changed the relationship between the UK's occult subculture and wider society.

But fascism is now knocking on the door in ways which would have seemed like the most dystopian of fantasies in the 80s. Now is the moment to review what we have learned from what has gone before in the sphere of magical resistance and take it to the barricades. Ecological collapse looms; the very right to exist for many of us is being eroded daily; everywhere, the blight of populism is apparent. They seek to befuddle and divide us, but in coming together, in making alliances with others, we can resist and overcome the oppressors who seek to draw us back into despair and darkness.

EARTH EMPOWERMENT

On 20th March 1992, between 10pm - Midnight, PaganLink Network is coordinating a mass raising of energy for the intention of *Earth Empowerment*. We wish to empower enthusiasm for Networking - to link hands across the Earth, so that by our shared vision, which is embracing the spirit of the Earth, we can bring about *change*. Power may be raised through meditation, dancing, chanting, prayer, ritual or celebration. Choose your favourite way of raising energy and join in!

Visualise the Networking symbol spinning deosil, and when your energy-raising 'peaks', send it spinning outwards, casting forth rays of fire flying out to link up with other people, irrespective of belief, creed, or colour - that we can join together, despite our differences, and find unity in our hearts. Feel the symbol empowering the Earth and connecting us together.

The Networking Symbol chosen denotes Fire - the fire of enthusiasm, motivation, and energy to promote action.

20th March
10pm-Midnight
Mars in Aquarius
Mercury in Aries.

Live your beliefs and act. Knowing that what you do will make a difference. This will turn the world around.

Please help by Photocopying, displaying or passing on this poster.

PaganLink Symbol designed by Chrys Livings. A Pagan News/PaganLink collaboration, 1992.
Thanks to Chaos International for scanning/typesetting assistance

11

Flyer for a PaganLink Mass Ritual event, 1992.

Moments and Movements of Magical Resistance

In the late 1970s, when I was taking my first faltering steps into the UK occult scene, magic in the service of politics was seen as sinister. Many of the magicians and witches I met held the view that magic and politics simply did not belong together—and if people *were* doing magic for political ends, it was indicative of being a black magician or on the Left-Hand Path. This view owed a great deal to the writings of Dion Fortune. For example, in *Psychic Self-Defence* (1930), Fortune states:

> I personally, am of the opinion that an occult fraternity is extremely ill-advised to concern itself with politics for reasons which I have stated in another of my books, *Sane Occultism*, and which I will not enter upon now, as they are not relevant to these pages.

Fortune makes veiled digs throughout *Psychic Self-Defence* against occult fraternities becoming involved in 'subversive' politics—particularly the lodges that she characterises as 'of dubious whiteness'.

In *Sane Occultism* (1929), Fortune writes:

> It may be argued that the occultist with his deeper insight is the natural leader of reform and should bear his part in social movements. I reply, let him be active in humanitarian efforts by all means but let him flee any interference in politics as he would the devil, for the experience of centuries has shown that it leads to nothing but trouble.

She goes on to assert that an occultist can be 'a teacher of spiritual things' or 'a leader in the affairs of the world' but certainly not both.

Most of the witches and pagans I met during the late 70s and early 80s were not interested in ecology or feminism, and if anything, were rather conservative in their outlook. Some cited the story that during the Battle of Britain in the Second World War, a mass gathering of witches had held a ritual to prevent Hitler invading Great Britain, but this was not seen as political in quite the same way. Yet there were occultists and pagans involved in forms of political activism who were actively using magic to further their aims—although I only found out about them once I'd moved beyond the local occult scene in my home town.

The view that occultism and politics should not be mixed started to change as the 1980s progressed. Here are some of the events and movements that moved the conversation about magical resistance onwards. This is a personal selection, so apologies if I have missed something out.

Greenham Common

The Peace Camp at Greenham Common (1981-2000) is probably the most famous UK event of magical resistance in the late twentieth century. It is now regularly cited as an example of radical witchcraft activism. It is often described as a woman-only camp, but in actuality this only applied to the Green Gate site—the other sites within the camp admitted men during the daylight hours. I wasn't really aware of what was going on until I began to meet women activists who'd been at the Camp in the mid-1980s. Some of them were involved in later actions such as Stop the City, the PaganLink mass rituals, and the Road Protests of the early 90s.

What kind of witches were at Greenham? According to Shai Ferraro's *Invoking Hecate at the Women's Peace Camp* (drawn from memoirs, archival records and insider interviews) the camp was a space where a heterogeneous mix of views were brought together, such as Goddess Feminists, Dianic Witches, New Age Travellers, and Feminists who rejected the concept of Spirituality entirely. Whilst the camp did receive enthusiastic support from some sections of the UK pagan community (notably Pagans Against Nukes, below), there were also tensions. Some UK pagans were very wary of feminism. A complaint I certainly recall hearing was that feminists didn't accept that the god-goddess binary of Wicca, and also, that men and women should be equal—and that feminism was therefore 'unbalanced'. Ferraro quotes Asphodel Long, saying that 'until American views started becoming important in the British Goddess scene, spiritual feminism and witchcraft or paganism hardly ever met. Spiritual feminists [in Britain] did not identify as witches until the early and mid-eighties and then only a minority did so. The work of Starhawk and Z. Budapest had a startling effect.' I agree. Starhawk's *Dreaming the Dark* lit a fire in me. Not only was it motivating, but Starhawk gave some very clear guidance on how magic could be used as a political tool. (Shai also explores the tensions between different forms of paganism and feminisms in *Women and Gender Issues in British Paganism, 1945-1990*.)

Pagans Against Nukes

Pagans Against Nukes (P.A.N) was formed in 1980 by Philip Cozens (aka Rufus Brock Maychild) and his partner, Kate. They founded P.A.N after attending an anti-Nuclear demonstration at Greenham before the Peace Camp was established. Together, they founded a magazine, *The Pipes of*

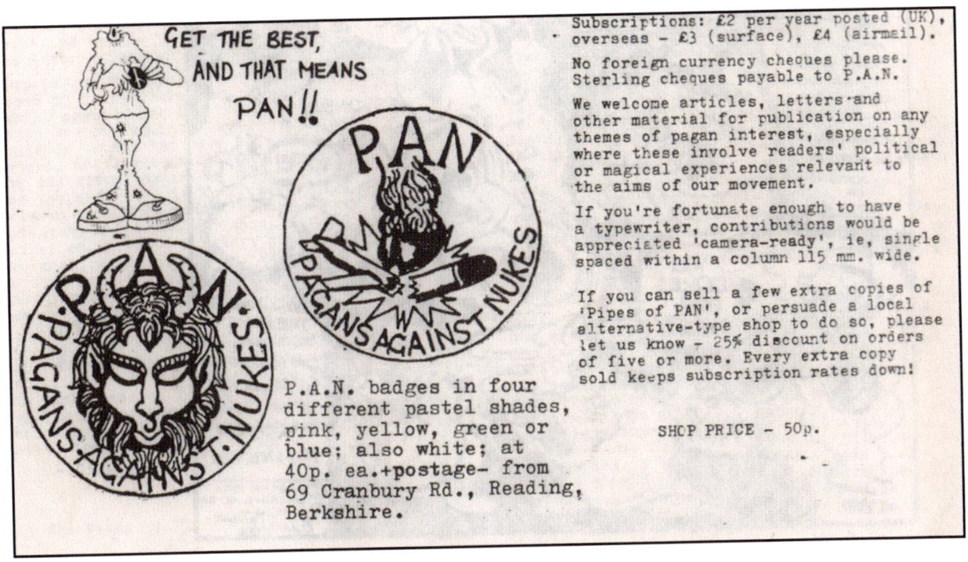
GET THE BEST, AND THAT MEANS PAN!!

P.A.N
PAGANS AGAINST NUKES

PAN
PAGANS AGAINST NUKES

P.A.N. badges in four different pastel shades, pink, yellow, green or blue; also white; at 40p. ea.+postage- from 69 Cranbury Rd., Reading, Berkshire.

Subscriptions: £2 per year posted (UK), overseas - £3 (surface), £4 (airmail).

No foreign currency cheques please. Sterling cheques payable to P.A.N.

We welcome articles, letters and other material for publication on any themes of pagan interest, especially where these involve readers' political or magical experiences relevant to the aims of our movement.

If you're fortunate enough to have a typewriter, contributions would be appreciated 'camera-ready', ie, single spaced within a column 115 mm. wide.

If you can sell a few extra copies of 'Pipes of PAN', or persuade a local alternative-type shop to do so, please let us know - 25% discount on orders of five or more. Every extra copy sold keeps subscription rates down!

SHOP PRICE - 50p.

Pipes of Pan cover and Pagans Against Nukes badges.

Stop the City flyer, 1983.

Pan, and distributed it through the few occult bookshops then operating across the UK. By 1983, *Pipes* had several hundred subscribers. Local P.A.N groups also sprang up around the country and members were active in organizing open meetings and rituals in various parts of the UK. P.A.N were involved in the Greenham protests and other counter-cultural movements of the period. In 1984, P.A.N organized the Earth Awareness Conference as a counter to what they saw as the increasing commercialization of the festival scene. The P.A.N network closed down in the early 1990s, as it was felt that the threat of impeding nuclear Armageddon had receded.

Stop the City

Between 1983-84 London saw several Stop the City actions. In the 1983 Stop the City actions, Kali, Eris and Hecate were invoked by participating magicians, and I know of at least two of them who had been at Greenham. Stop the City had no central organizers, although anarchists from the London Greenpeace group helped to initiate it. The idea was very much that people should organize their own protests.

PaganLink

In the mid-1980s, many of the debates about magic and political action took place through the zines and meetings of PaganLink Network. A proper history of PaganLink is yet to be written. It did much to revitalise the UK's pagan scene in the mid-1980s and early 1990s, through a series of conferences both large and small, organising local moots, outdoor events and a proliferation of 'zines and newsletters. Rich Westwood, one of the founders of PaganLink, published *Moonshine* magazine eight times a year. Several free, small regional newsletters also sprang up: among them *Northern PaganLink News*, edited by myself and Rodney Orpheus.

PaganLink's audience was a new generation of people who loosely defined themselves as Pagans without necessarily being initiated witches or magicians. It was an uneasy alliance of groups with sometimes very different perspectives on life, the universe and everything. Anarchist Pagans brushed up against Wiccans who believed in hierarchies and polarity. There were New Age Travellers, Hippies and self-styled urban shamans.

PaganLink did much to revitalize the loose network of regular 'pagan moots' up and down the country, many of which had ceased to meet as former organizers had stepped away. PaganLink created a loose network of area coordinators: people who were willing to have their names and contact details listed in Pagan 'zines and posted on shop noticeboards. These volunteers were encouraged to start up local moots and do anything they felt necessary to support Pagans in their locality. It wasn't always successful. Sometimes for example, it would emerge that a person who had volunteered to be a local organizer was not a popular choice for a large segment of the local community. There were frequent arguments about the future direction and organization of the network. Efforts to create a commonly-held Pagan Manifesto or a Council of Elders failed, although they led to spirited debates. Thirty years on, some people are still arguing about their various projects and the lack of general support for them.

One of PaganLink's first publications to directly address 'political paganism' was Rich Westwood's and John Walbridge's *Awakening the Dragon: Practical Paganism, Political Ritual and Active Ecology* (1988) that argued, forcefully, that Paganism and political action were inseparable and made a direct challenge to what they termed 'spare bedroom paganism'. Although much of the text has not aged well—some of the authors' views on history, politics, economics and gender, for example, would, I think, be considered hopelessly naive nowadays, *Awakening the Dragon*, with its thoughts on Pagan ethical living, networking, community building, urban shamanism, envisioning possible futures and suggested formats for 'mass ritual' was still ground-breaking and inspiring:

> By declaring ourselves Pagan, we have stepped out of the mainstream of society, and to a certain extent put ourselves on the line both materially and spiritually. … We maybe need to take the lead from such as "Pagans Against Nukes" or "Pagan Animal Rights" or from the Political Paganism described in Starhawk's *Dreaming the Dark*. Or are we content to be spare bedroom witches? … We have to take our internal knowings and manifest them. We cannot sit on the fence. For soon they will replace it with razor wire and it won't be so comfortable then.

Rich Westwood and John Walbridge were also sharply critical of occult practitioners whose practice was entirely focused on spiritual development:

> Golden Dawnies, Crowley arse kissers and the rest ... developing their own selves, contacting Guardian Angels etc., and are not involved, in a holistic sense, with the overall health of the planet.

They also raised the issue of how to live a magical life in an urban environment, and suggested that the public jingoism encouraged by the government during the Falklands War was a magical act.

Although many PaganLink activists had concerns about impending ecological collapse, there was also a shared anger over what Margaret Thatcher's Conservative Government had done to the country. Pagans might have thought themselves unaffected by the year-long miner's strike or by Clause 28, but the Battle of the Beanfield in 1985 showed that no one was safe. The Battle of the Beanfield took place when over a thousand police prevented the Peace Convoy from holding a free festival at Stonehenge.

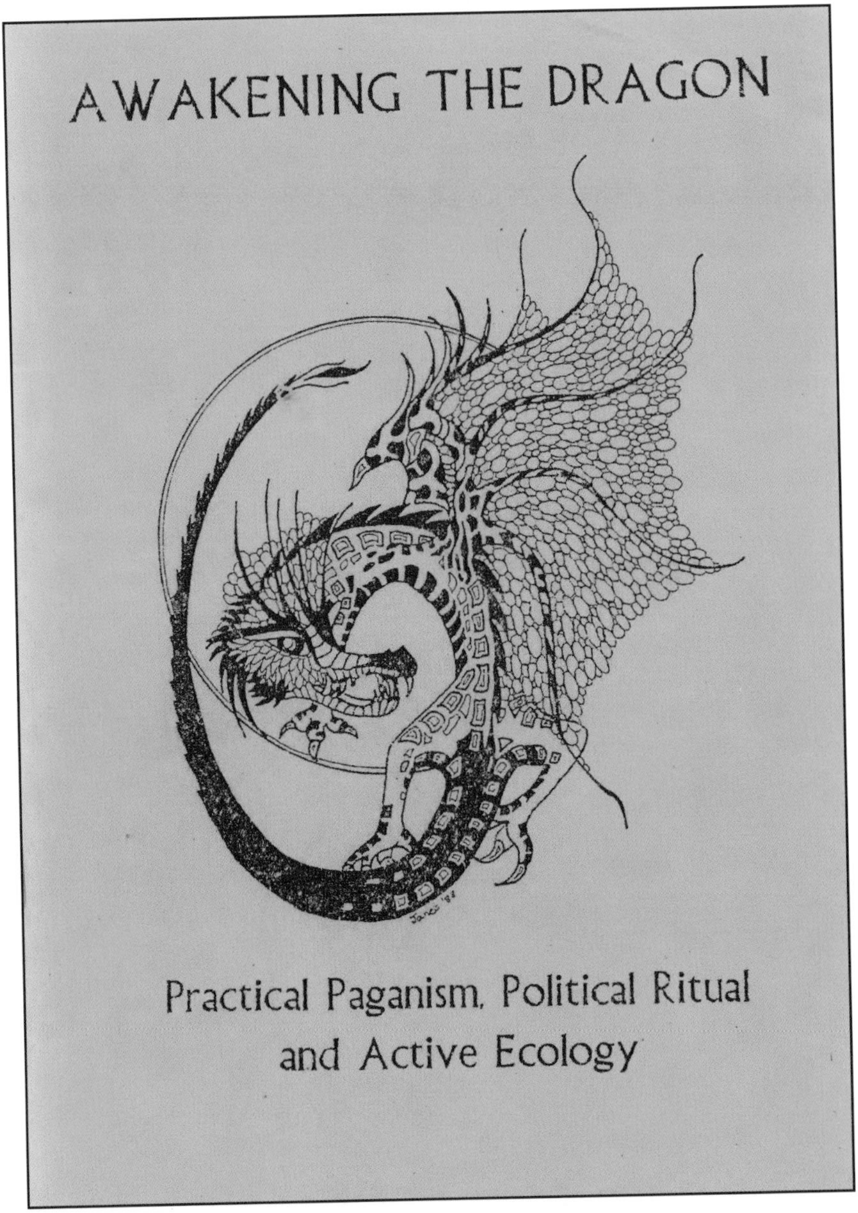

Awakening the Dragon (1988) by Rich Westwood and John Walbridge.

PaganLink Regional Newsletters.

Over 500 people were arrested—one of the largest mass arrests in English history. There was a definite sense that, even without the 'Satanic Panic' which was then just kicking off, alternative lifestyles were under threat.

It was PaganLink participants which kicked off a new enthusiasm in the UK for mass rituals: events, group and solo participants joining together all at a particular time and day—the Summer Solstice for example—in order to raise energy or at least awareness of particular issues.

The Road Protests and Dragon

In the early 1990s a conversation started on the subject of Ecomagick, largely inspired by the activities of the Dragon Environmental Network: magic inspired not only to protect the land but also to empower those who were activists. Dragon was formed by Adrian Harris in 1990:

> Respect and care for the Earth is an integral part of many spiritual paths, particularly shamanism and witchcraft. Yet too few of us are active in ecology in our everyday practice: I suggest forming a group combining campaigning and ritual to heal the Earth. Some may be drawn more to one or the other, but strength lies in this combination: magical ritual is our spirit—campaign action keeps us grounded to earth.

By 1996 there were 13 local Dragon Groups, over 300 active members, and a quarterly newsletter. Dragon also organized workshops and conferences. Dragon were involved in supporting several high-profile actions such as the Twyford Down protests of 1992; the M11 Link Road Campaign, where bailiffs, backed by a large number of police, battled protesters who were guarding a 250-year-old chestnut tree. (The tree was torn down in December 1993.) Dragon also worked with the Freedom Network to raise Pagan awareness of the implications of the Criminal Justice Bill in 2003.

During the road protests, sigils of breakdown were spray-painted on bulldozers; charms and talismans hung on barbed wire. Magical practitioners of different traditions and approaches put aside their differences and came together to support campaigns to save Oxleas Woods and other areas. Some joined activists squatting the land, preventing it from being developed; others concentrated on keeping people informed about developments and working to gain the support and trust of local residents.

There was much debate over the politics of power over vs. empowerment, or—from the chaos kids in particular—whether it was useful to magically attack institutions rather than individuals; or to try and send share prices tumbling down.

In 1999, Dragon released *The Dragon Guide to Campaigning Ecomagick*—a free PDF ebook available from the Dragon website (see

Further Reading). In addition to giving tips on rituals, the Guide gives some very useful advice on how to begin campaigning; facilitating meetings; dealing with the media and Non-Violent Direct Action.

In 2004, Adrian Harris and Sean Scullion released another free ebook: an *Introduction to Pagan Activism*, ahead of the G8 protests in 2005 (also available from the Dragon website). Harris & Scullion wrote of a 'Pagan Cluster' at the forthcoming G8 protests who would work 'with the intention of intensifying the strength of non-violent protest and causing disruption to those who would rule and plunder our world.' They also suggested that Pagan Activisms could include magic to protect protesters from injury or arrest; invocations of Eris the and her apple of Chaos; offering healing support to protesters and using runes to charge protest letters.

Pagans against the Poll Tax

In 1990 the conservative government introduced a new system of local taxation; a head tax that every citizen had to pay to their local authority. This Community Charge quickly became known as the Poll Tax. It was introduced in Scotland and Wales in 1989, and implemented across the rest of the UK in 1990. In the early months of 1990, thousands of anti Poll Tax demonstrations and actions mushroomed across the country. Some of these demonstrations became riots, with police using horses and baton charges in an attempt to disperse demonstrators. The largest demonstration took place on 31st March in London, with over 200,000 people attending.

Amongst the protests and actions there were some who looked towards magical solutions. One of my friends in Leeds for example, came up with the idea of changing his name to 'Delete File' in the hope that overworked council staff, seeing that flash up on the screen, would automatically delete his records. He didn't actually do this, but I thought it was a novel approach. Another suggestion came from an anonymously-circulation document from a group calling themselves Pagans against the Poll Tax. Their suggestion was simple. Citing the old wart-charmer trick of buying warts from a sufferer and transferring them somewhere else, they suggested that the transfer of money could transfer other things as well. They recommended using a cheque—appropriately decorated with magical symbols, made to pay a local council with 'six months of computer trouble', or anything that might hinder the collection of the Poll Tax. They made the point that even if the curse cheque didn't have a magical effect, council staff opening an envelope containing it might be freaked out at such a reception.

Lawrence Burton's account of the Levitation of Parliament by members of TOPY -1
Reproduced with permission.

Lawrence Burton's account of the Levitation of Parliament by members of TOPY -2
Reproduced with permission.

Anarchy in the UK

Between 21-30 October 1994, London was the venue for the massive Anarchy in the UK festival; a wide range of disparate counter-cultural groups combining their efforts, with no central organisers, to celebrate and protest. There was a huge array of events, from political meetings to poetry readings; from street theatre to workshops on every conceivable subject, from astrology to class war. One of the highlights was the attempt, led by members of the Temple of Psychic Youth (TOPY) to levitate the Houses of Parliament, on 27 October.

TOPY members later took part in the mass protests in London and Manchester in the wake of the Operation Spanner trial. Operation Spanner was a police action against a group of gay men who were part of the UK's then largely underground S&M culture. As a result of the operation, a number of videos showing men engaged in sadomasochistic practices were seized, and 16 men were sent to trial. Despite their pleading that the practices they had engaged in were consensual and conducted in private with safe words, and that no one had ever been injured, it was ruled that consent, in this case did not count and the men were sentenced to various lengths of imprisonment. The case was not fully dismissed until February 2009, by the European Court of Human Rights. In the early 90s, members of TOPY ran a lengthy campaign to close down a Dolphinarium in Brighton.

Anti-Fracking Activisms

Fracking—hydraulic fracturing is a method by which gas or oil is extracted from shale rock. Since 2010, the British government have been permitting companies to open up drilling sites, some of which are adjacent to national parks. Many people are concerned about the environmental and social impact of fracking, and many pagans and occult practitioners are organizing and building alliances in order to protest and support anti-fracking activisms.

In 2013 for example, the Bolton Area Pagans held an hour-long protest ceremony, joining with pagans in other parts of the world, to protest against fracking. In 2014, a group calling itself The Warrior's Call: Pagans United against Fracking emerged to support anti-fracking protests. Again, like many other movements discussed in this book, it has no central organization and makes no distinctions between different pagan faiths or traditions. Anyone can join and organize their own local group. The Warrior's Call has allied with Frack Free Lancashire—a loose coalition of anti-fracking groups protesting fracking sites across the county.

QueerWolf

A RADICAL SPIRITUALITY NETWORK

CONTACT:

QueerWolf is a London–based Radical Spirituality Network for Gay Men, Lesbians & Bisexuals who are interested in exploring alternative forms of spiritual paths – particularly Paganism & the Occult. Weird? Not really. Contrary to the lies spread in the media, the Occult is not one long round of orgies & baby–eating – any more than the well–worn fables that are constantly dredged up against Lesbians & Gay men. Since the beginning of this century, there has been a great increase of interest in alternative religions & lifestyles, and we have found that more and more people are becoming interested in exploring ways of living that can be loosely typified as Pagan or Occult – Magick, Shamanism, Witchcraft, & Voudou being just a few examples.

Why? The mass religions that have dominated our culture are strongly homophobic, pleasure–denying, and impose a moral code of conduct which must be obeyed. Anyone who dares to be different is scapegoated as a heretic. In contrast, Pagan & Occult philosophies stress that morality 'grows from within', that diversity & differences are to be valued, and life is to be enjoyed, rather than suffered.

We have been led to believe that to be 'spiritual' means being not quite of this world. But Pagan & Occult lifestyles are intensely pragmatic – involving techniques of adjusting & adapting to the world more successfully – both individually and collectively.

We take a radical stance in that we are open to the possibilities inherent in these alternatives – many of which have been supressed or dismissed by deliberate ridicule. We want to uncover the 'Queer Myths' that feature in different cultures and examine the ways in which non–Western societies deal with same–sex love. We celebrate the fact of individual diversity as a strength, our sexuality as a joy, and our lifestyle as a celebration of inner power.

Why QueerWolf? A name chosen because we are twice–damned by 'straight' society – heretics due to our sexuality, and because we embrace the heresy of a magical universe. A few hundred years ago we would have been burnt at the stake – the Church saw both homosexuality & Witchcraft as acts inspired by 'the Devil' and popular belief had it that 'sodomites' were born from the copulations of witches. Some religious fundamentalists would no doubt wish that these beliefs were revived – and when you consider that many 'top' Tories combine ingrained homophobia with a belief in the 'evil' of Witchcraft, you don't need crystal balls to see which way the wind is blowing. Queer encompasses our diversity and the unescapable fact that most people – gay and straight, see us as 'weird'. Wolf because we are individuals who choose to gather together, to howl, prowl and explore. 'QueerWolf' – from 'WereWolf' – as we are shape shifters, creatures of the night, explorers of the uncanny.

Queerwolf - London Queer Activist 'zine from 1992.

Magic in the aid of political protest continues in the UK. Only recently (January 2023) there were reports in regional newspapers that supporters of the campaign to keep wild camping on Dartmoor had conducted rituals and ceremonies as part of the protests; calling on the spirit of 'Old Crockern', the ancient genius loci of the moors.

Queer Magical Activism

Queer Magical Activisms have a long history, particularly in the U.S.A. In 1970, for example, the Los Angeles Gay Liberation Front, in response to police violence, performed an action, the intent of which was to use magick to levitate and temporarily disappear the local police precinct. Attendees were asked to bring tin cans and pencils to bang them with: which the organizers hoped would make 'an ominous and interesting sound'.

North America has, for the most part, led the way when it comes to Queer Magical Activism. In no small way, this is largely thanks to Leo Martello (1930-2000), a founder member of the Gay Liberation Front and a public witch who sought recognition for his beliefs. The author of two books: *Weird Ways of Witchcraft* (1972) and *Witchcraft: The Old Religion* (1973), Martello also contributed to *ComeOut!*, the first publication of the Gay Liberation Movement. Here, courtesy of Brooke Palmieri, is Leo Martello in a fiery mood:

> My curses for 1970 are: I curse all those who have hounded and harassed homosexuals simply as a result of their own sex hangups with having sons who turn out homosexual. I curse all those who exploit the gay power -movement in order to promote other non-gay ideologies to get exactly what they deserve: Contempt. I curse all those who support the Vietnam War with lifelong guilt. May they personally suffer the consequences of their support. I curse all those pseudo-patriotic parents who back the Vietnam War and government's policies. (If their sons return home in coffins let them realize how they sanctioned the murder of their own sons by their own ideology.)
>
> I curse all those public officials who vote against repeal of the sodomy laws with discovering sodomites in their own families. I curse all those black-robed sexually hungup judges who mete out unjust prison terms to homosexuals with having their hearts literally turn to stone.
>
> I place a HEX On the SEX lives of all those who use their gay brothers and sisters to promote totalitarian philosophies, whether of the Far Left or the Far Right. I curse all those pseudo he-man hunters of innocent animals with lifelong impotence. I curse all those parents who have rejected and disowned their gay sons and daughters with having their neighbors discover their children's homosexuality. I curse all racist bigots with a breakdown.

There was no one in the UK remotely like Martello. The UK's pagan scene was, for the most part, unwelcoming towards people who weren't straight (a subject I write about more fully in my book *Queering Occultures*). There were, of course, LGBTQ Pagans and occultists, but few were publicly 'out' and vocal, and there wasn't much in the way of pagan networking going on until HOBLink network emerged in the 1980s, and later, small activist/support groups such as the London-based Queerwolf in the early 1990s.

A history of Queer Magical Activisms in the UK is yet to be written. The UK's Queer Pagan Camp (QPC) had close associations with the D.I.Y culture that had emerged in the queer squats of London (in particular, Brixton) and elsewhere. This 'Do It Yourself' ethos owed much to the Queeruption movement, and was expressed through zines such as *AnarQuist* that explored the affinities between Queer activism and anarchism. The first issue of *AnarQuist* featured extracts from Arthur Evan's classic *Witchcraft and the Gay Counterculture*. Not only did QPC challenge heteronormative Paganism, there was also a strong element of eco-activism and using magic to support radical social change. All decision-making was done on a consensus basis, and anyone could turn up and offer a workshop, such as the memorable 'Enlightenment through Lipstick'. The Queer Pagan Camp vision statement says:

The Queer Pagan Camp banner at an anti-war demo.
With thanks to Lou Hart.

Established in 1998, QPC works on the basis of respect; for ourselves, each other, the Land, the Spirits, Animals, the Planet, the Folk (also called Faery), the Mysteries and Deities. As Queer Pagans we come from a variety of pagan paths and from all forms of gender identity and consensual sexuality. If you are lesbian, gay, bisexual, trans (LGBT), heterosexual, gender-queer, asexual, non- binary – however you identify you will be welcome here. We also look at our pagan practices from a queer perspective – exploring and creating queer myths and mysteries and challenging those practices which do not fit our queer pagan, earth-honouring values.

Some lessons from the Squat Scene

I also learnt a great deal about activism from being around friends who were squatting in parts of Leeds during the late 1980s. Leeds Squatters Network came about via a group of people who had the idea of squatting a large building in the city centre, as a protest to highlight lack of housing and community facilities. It was during the Miners Strike, at the peak of the Thatcher years, and the group were united by the common experience of political & social alienation. With a few exceptions, most of the group had no experience of squatting or political actions. Their first meetings were advertised through the University, leafleting various gigs, and through the London-based Squatter's magazine, *Crowbar*. Out of the group's first action—the squatting of Leeds Rates building, evolved the Leeds Squatter's Network, which in tum, developed various spin-offs. These included: a housing co-op (housing over 12 people), a food co-op that ran a whole food delivery service, and a street theatre group that put on public performances.

The Network also gave a boost to the local Claimants Union, which, together with Scottish Claimants Unions, went on to initiate the National Campaign against the Poll Tax; Leeds University Hunt Sabs were given more support, and a non-University group was set up, making both groups more dynamic. A band promotions group was formed to hold weekly gigs and occasional benefit concerts; three women's groups sprang from the Network: Women's Action on Benefits, Maternity Emergency (a benefits advice group) and Girls in Need (which campaigned to set up a hostel for runaway girls).

A women's only squat was opened; five large buildings in the city centre were squatted for benefit gigs; a 'squat cafe' flourished briefly, and there was a wide variety of political occupations & demonstrations including Leeds' own version of Stop The City. A tools co-op was created, and a shared-skills network so that people could get their houses re-wired and re-plumbed. In addition, publications were issued such as *Who Owns Leeds*, and *Cabaret* (a collection of situationist agit-prop).

This buzz of activity was helped along by a weekly 'zine, *No Limits*. It's great attraction (that got people reading it) was that it published the weeks' TV listings from the *Radio & TV Times*. *No Limits* was run on an 'anybody who wants to do it, does it' basis, though eventually, this devolved to a team of about eight people who produced the 'zine on a rotating basis. No one knew everyone else's address, but there was a team who were responsible for picking it up and distributing it within their own postal area.

Within Leeds Squatters Network, there were no leaders as such—people may have been responsible for one particular task, but they had no leadership status outside it, something that consistently confused the authorities. Through a box number, the Network connected nationally with other Squatters Networks, and with Anarchist groups, Women's groups, Animal Rights activists, and Travellers.

What I found particularly interesting was how people became involved with the Network. Due to the clandestine nature of many of the Network's activities, there was never any publishing of names and addresses, nor was there any central database of same. People joined the Network entirely through personal introductions and social gatherings. Only in the case of very large events, were they advertised in advance. *No Limits* publicised what people had done—not what they were thinking of doing (for obvious reasons).

After talking to people who'd been involved with the Squatters Network at various points, I was amazed by what they had achieved. I also began to see some key points emerging. A crucial point is that most of the people involved in the Network were homeless, and shared the same political stance. This gave them a common commitment perhaps lacking in Pagan circles—where people are often suspicious of each other's beliefs and motivations. Another key point is that the network quickly evolved into a multiplicity of groups all exchanging information & support with each other. There were weekly meetings where people would pool information and resources. Specialists came in and shared their skills with others. To do this, a Network needs to be small, and highly adaptive. Also, the continual stream of events; actions, gigs, the weekly newsletter; all helped people feel they were engaged in something 'busy'.

Acts of Enchantment

Here's a brief romp through a variety of approaches to magical activism; drawing, where possible, on my own experiences.

Mass Ritual

One development in the 1980s was the organisation of Mass Rituals.

- What's important for me about Mass Rituals are these points:
- They draw people together for a common goal.
- They help foster a sense of communal purpose between different groups of practitioners.
- They help create and support local activist networks.
- Their enactment, regardless of any immediate or observable effect helps participants feel certain that they can make a difference.

Heal the Earth was a mass ritual, aimed at getting people in different localities to perform a ritual or magical act (we didn't specify what form it should be) on the day of the Summer Solstice, 1987, between 12 and 2pm in the aid of raising people's awareness of the global ecological crisis. It was felt that rather than giving people a set ritual to perform, we'd leave what people did up to them.

We discussed the idea of specific political issues, but in the end decided to aim for a general raising of awareness: 'a ripple across the human planetary mind' as one person put it. I don't want to claim sole responsibility for this action, but I did learn some very important lessons in helping to get it off the ground, principally, that other people's enthusiasm was essential in gathering impetus for getting a project off the ground. Just being in a group of people throwing ideas around was a great experience, and then taking those ideas to other groups, and feeling their enthusiasm too was wonderful. Sheila Broun, a local magical artist and teacher, let us use an image she'd done of the Ace of Cups as an image to focus on, and we worded the leaflet in order to make it as succinct as possible. The leaflets were displayed in shops, snuck into books and magazines, and distributed at festivals up and down the country. The Leeds group alone distributed about 7,000 leaflets—not bad for people mostly on low incomes, and we later found out that over 20,000 had been distributed. Was the ritual a success? That I don't know, and anyway, I think it is not helpful to make claims about such things. What was important for me though, was more or less the doing of it; the talking to people; being spurred on by their enthusiasm and support.

Heal the Earth was repeated in 1990 as Listen to the Earth. This time around, some activists organized gigs for local bands, using the focus sigil as a stage backdrop. Once again, there was no formal ritual outline, and participants were encouraged to do whatever they felt was appropriate.

My own feeling is that these kind of events should be "one offs" as it were, and that if they are repeated over time they lose intensity and become routinised. Personally, I feel that getting people together in groups to do stuff—if only to dance and drum, is more effective than participants sitting alone in their bedrooms meditating on a symbol.

HEAL THE EARTH

On the Summer Solstice (Sunday June 21) between Mid-day and 2pm there will be a mass raising of energy aimed at increasing Ecological Awareness. The power of directed and focused energy raised by meditation, chanting, dancing, music, prayer, ritual, or any kind of celebration will help to raise awareness of our Global Ecological crisis, and so promote change, in accordance with our visions THE ACE OF CUPS IS THE SYMBOL CHOSEN TO HELP EACH PERSON OR GROUP INVOLVED TO FOCUS THEIR THOUGHTS _ TO JOIN THE FLOW OF ENERGY.

The Ace of Cups Symbolises the power of Love. Creativity, and nurturing Growth

ACE OF CUPS SHEILA BROUN 1486

"Under Heaven nothing is more soft and yielding than water, Yet for attacking the Solid and Strong, nothing is better. It has no equal "

LAO_TZU TAO TE CHING

Please help this endeavour by adding your power to the flow Thoughts are like water- a few drops may pass unnoticed, but enough drops flowing together become a River In celebration at the Solstice, we can let our energies flow together to become a great wave of power, aimed and focused This will help raise awareness. and so promote the changes neccesary to our survival

"Live your Beliefs and act. knowing that
what you can do will make a difference.
This will turn the World around "
Thoreau

Please help by Displaying, Passing on, Or Copying this Leaflet - thanks

Heal the Earth flyer 1987

LISTEN TO THE EARTH

One of the **LISTEN TO THE EARTH** projects will take place on **April 9th 1990, (Full Moon Rising) between 9pm and 11pm.** ***Pagan News*** will be co-ordinating a mass raising of energy, with the intention of increasing awareness of Ecological issues, and how we can promote change in accordance with our ideals. Power may be raised by meditation, dancing, chanting, music, prayer, ritual or any kind of celebration, so choose your favourite way of raising power and join in! THE ACE OF CUPS IS THE SYMBOL CHOSEN TO ALLOW EVERYONE PARTICIPATING TO FOCUS THEIR ENERGIES INTO THE FLOW.

The Ace of Cups symbolises the power of Love, Inspiration, Creativity, Ideals and Nurturing Growth.

9 APRIL, 9-11PM, FULL MOON RISING

FULL MOON 10 APRIL, 4.20am.

Moon 20⁰ Libra

Under Heaven nothing is more soft and yielding than water,

Yet for attacking the solid and strong, nothing is better.

It has no equal.

Lao-Tzu, Tao Te Ching

Please help our endeavour by adding your energy to the flow. Thoughts are like water - a few drops may pass unnoticed, but enough of them flowing together becomes a river. In celebrating together, we can focus our energie so that we create a great wave of power, reaching out across the world. Our aim is to raise awareness of Ecological issues, and so promote the changes neccesary to ensure the survival and recovery of our world.

9pm

Live your beliefs and act. Knowing that what you do will make a difference. This will turn the world around.

11pm

PLEASE HELP BY DISPLAYING, PASSING ON, OR COPYING THIS POSTER

Ace of Cups image by *Sheila Broun*

9

Listen to the Earth Flyer.

The Black Djinn Curse

I first read Hakim Bey's Black Djinn Curse in *Nox*. No.4—a small zine dealing with chaos magic and other "sinister" trajectories. It was a simple idea—cursing institutions rather than individuals.

The Curse is simple:

Send the company a package containing a bottle, corked & sealed with black wax. Inside: dead insects, scorpions, lizards & the like.

A bag containing graveyard dirt along with other noxious substances; an egg pierced with iron nails & pins, and a scroll on which is drawn a yantra or 'veve'.

This invokes the Black Djinn, the Dark Shadow.

An accompanying note should explain that this hex is against institutions & not individuals. But unless the institution itself ceases to be malign, the curse, like a mirror, will begin to infect the premises with noxious fortune—a miasma of negativity.

Prepare a 'news release' explaining the curse & taking credit for it in the name of some invented society. Send copies to all employees in the institution & selected media. The night before these arrive, wheat paste the premises of the institution with copies of the Black Djinn emblem where they will be seen by all employees arriving for work the next morning.

Admittedly, I never tried this out myself, but it set me thinking nonetheless about different possibilities for magical resistance against oppressive forces.

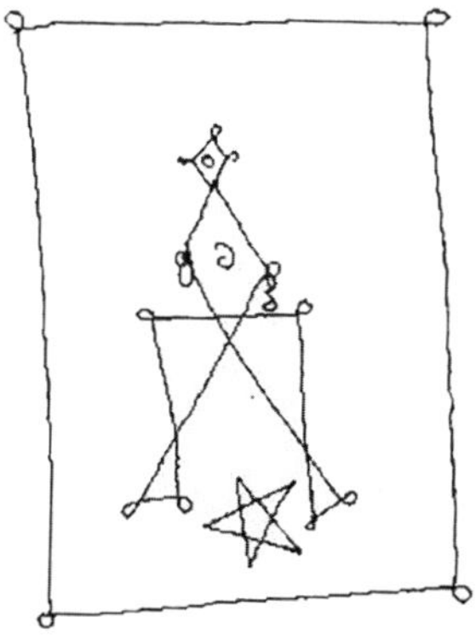

Supporting Activisms

For purposes of discussion, I suggest 2 general approaches to supporting activisms—direct involvement and Support actions.

Direct involvement is easy enough—it's when magical practitioners are themselves directly involved in protests and other activism. But what might constitute a Support Action? Here's a few examples:

Servitor in a Teapot

I visited a group of friends in Wales who were engaged in eco-actions. They were interested in magical support for their work. We discussed what approaches might suit them best, and one thing that came up was that their discussions often petered out without firm decisions or devolved into argument. Eventually we decided to create a servitor that lived in a teapot, it's object being to both generate ideas and to help agreements take shape. The servitor was activated by simply pouring out tea in a group meeting. We did a fun ritual to create the servitor, and that was that.

Cutting webs of power

Scene: meeting of Leeds Anti-Fascist-Action, some time in 1986:

> "Okay, I've been asked to come and facilitate a magical action. I know some of you are very sceptical about this, which is okay by me. Feel free not to participate. You might think it's all a bit silly. You could just think of it like some of the Agit-Prop stuff Danbert and co. did in the town centre a couple of years back. A lark, nothing more.
>
> So … you won't mind then when I ask you to meditate on the swastika…."

'Scenes'—you know, the 'pagan scene', the 'squat scene'—whatever alternative communities you care to name; are at their most interesting, I think, at the points where they overlap or intersect. In the centres, people are perhaps a tad more predictable, or at least more easily stereotyped – whether it's the black-clad boys 'n' girls with their first edition Kenneth Grant books or the hardcore squatters who -in the week I arrived in Leeds—were still glorying in the riot up at the University after the Crisis UK gig. It's perhaps hard to see past the surface sometimes. Yer hardcore squatter, like the guy who told me (with evident pride) that he'd put a paving stone through the windshield of a police car would never be interested in magic, would he? Turns out I was wrong. There was plenty to do for someone with a small talent for sorcery or (much later) an urban shaman. Tarot readings for people with upcoming court cases; poking around rumoured haunted squat cellars; dowsing for the odd bit of sticky black lost in the folds of the settee. Small acts of sorcery; although I was never in quite the same league as the two women who helped out with speeding Dole claims through DHSS red tape, or 'Picklock Pete' whose expertise was often required to open up an empty house. But it was through my willingness to do anything, anywhere, in exchange for the occasional cooked meal or spliff, that I navigated my way through the loosely-interconnected dissident groups throughout the city: the hunt sabs people, the Atari ST hackers; rogue astrologists, alt.pagans who hewed to no recognisable tradition. And eventually to Anti-Fascist Action, who, somewhat to my surprise, did keep tabs on the UK occult scene—or at least those individuals who were rumoured to be ex-League of St. George or Combat 18.

I can't recall exactly what came next in the cutting webs event. Probably some brief blurb about the pagan antecedents of the Swastika. But the meditation was simple enough; we visualised the local fascists as having spread a sticky web of influence across the city, and some of us gave some examples. I'd recently had a missive from the so-called Brotherhood of Albion who proclaimed that whilst Hindus and Muslims were allowed to have their own temples, Pagans weren't, and indeed, were being hounded by the press. It wasn't hard to see where this had come from, and that the local British National Party were interested in sucking as many people under their greasy wings as possible. So we brought this sticky web of snot into our minds, and visualised a razor-edged whirling swastika slicing through it, the strands falling back, its weavers exposed and broken.

Leeds' vibrant and active dissident scene taught me some important lessons. Firstly, that you don't get a reputation for doing stuff by announcing yourself as an expert. There'd already been several instances of 'proper Pagans' turning up at traveller festivals in the UK and attempting to show people 'how to do rituals properly'. That went down as well as can be expected. You do stuff, you learn to be sensitive to people and places, and above all *listen*. Largely I found that people were more likely to share their experiences and thoughts on the weird if I wasn't overly credulous. They weren't afraid of having their experiences dismissed, but were more wary of the 'hello trees, hello sky' Paganism that invested far too much significance in the everyday weird. Secondly, that shared enthusiasm; the kind generated when small groups of people come together and get excited can carry you a long way, and fire any kind of project—from mass, country-wide ritual events to setting up a Pagan 'zine on zero budget, both projects I participated in during my stay in the city.

I'd like to be able to report that our little ritual had positive effects in pushing back right-wing influence in Leeds; that it had a tangible result. Actually, no. Even if that had been the case, that wouldn't have been important or really worth mentioning. I've always found people's claims that their ritual has led to some major seismic social event to be embarrassing, if not downright hubris. I can't remember if there was a tangible, or at least generously attributable outcome we could point to. That was almost besides the point. What was more important is that a bunch of people came together & acted or maybe just had a good time, maybe stretched their boundaries a bit.

Raising Anger

There is much talk of 'raising energy' but I have often found helping people to articulate and express their anger to be most effective.

Here's an example of an Anger-raising ritual performed at an ecomagick workshop. It was conceived as part of a thought-experiment for a movement called Gaia's Children. The intention was to get as far away as possible from the legacies of the nineteenth-century—transcendence of the everyday; chopping the world into divisions of high vs. low; spirit vs. mundane. Instead, we imagined a magical ethos which stressed, at every opportunity, the perspective that humanity is inextricably enmeshed in complex and ever-evolving networks: social, cultural, ecological. To take active stances of resistance.

The Earth Surge

This short ritual is structured around identification with four Goddesses - *Litha* (from Lithosphere - Earth), *Hydra* (Hydrosphere - Water), *Atma* (Atmosphere - Air) and *Bia* (Biosphere - Fire). Diverging from traditional magical ideas of human Goddesses, or the traditional associations of the elements, we took these four ecosystems as entities within the global Ecosystem - Gaia.

Participants begin kneeling on the ground. Drum begins slow pulse-beat (Heartbeat of Gaia).

Feel a slow rumbling deep in earth beneath you, at the base of your spine. Feel the slow power of Litha - tectonic plates grinding, the slow drift of continents, the power and presence of the rocks, mountains. Bring back the sensations & images of Litha.

Feel the surging of water, the rolling waves, the deep currents of the Ocean, the tides, and the blood surging around your body. Bring back the feelings of Hydra - the waters of life and death.

(Begin to stand up)

Feel the rushing of the air, the power of the winds, swirling currents and hurricanes. Bring back the power of Atma as you breathe in and out, feeling the air move through your lungs.

(Tilt your head back, begin to quicken breathing)

Feel the teeming presence of billions of life-forms: insects, plants, animals - the heat this generates is the heat of your body: in life, in cellular decay, in feeding and dying, in reproducing, in killing. Feel the power and energy of Bia - the totality of all life within GAIA.

Feel the world around you with a billion eyes and antennae, feel the flashes of pain as the earth is ripped open, as schools of fish die in the maw of factory trawlers. All your senses are attuned to what is happening within your body. Cancerous growths eat at your cells. The natural Chaos of Gaia's being is being concreted over: ripped apart and churned into chemical sludge. The poison is in your bones, in your blood, in the air which rushes through you, and it is destroying the delicate balances of the teeming life within you.

Images of mass destruction flash into your awareness: pollution, deliberate waste, the plundering of your body for a fast buck. The power within you begins to surge into a raging fury. Let a low rumbling sound of anger escape from your mouths....

(Begin to hyperventilate - low moaning)

Reach outwards into your body - find the small, scurrying beings who are causing you this pain - send your tendrils coursing into their mind - and there! Some of them want to stop what is happening. They feel for your hurt, but they lack vision - they lack resolve, they lack anger. Show them visions of how they can act, and send your power, your anger into them....

(All present link arms)

You are yourself, you are Gaia. Nature's Chaos surges through you. Linked to others, you know them as separate entities, linked by common purpose. Focus your mind on what YOU would like to achieve. Feel the power of Gaia surging through you. Images of pollution and the rape of the earth, torture and maiming for profit. Senseless acts everywhere.

Focus your mind on your desire and SCREAM WE ARE NOT TAKING ANY MORE SHIT!

(All collapse to the ground)

Another version of this kind of Anger-raising was created by some lesbian friends—they called it 'The Scream': visualising women of all races, in all cultures, in all eras, who have been oppressed, screaming their frustration and anger into the night.

Unleashing the Furies

The year, 1989. The place: Headingley, Leeds 6. It was a long hot summer, and gradually, tensions were rising. We suspected that the current dope famine was turning people to booze and speed (never a good combination, and this seemed to us to be manifesting in two ways) increasing incidents of queer-bashing and overt homophobia, and more reports of young women —particularly single mothers—being verbally abused and physically threatened. Headingley was changing; more heroin was coming into the area, and tensions becoming more apparent.

Living in Leeds 6 provided, for me, a unique opportunity to explore the possibilities offered by acting as a magical worker in an urban community. At the time, Headingley had a large alternative population (over 70% of housing was given over to multi-occupancy dwelling) consisting of students, squatters, self-defined anarchists and people living on the dole or participating in the black economy. There was a strong feeling of community - and, as in any community, there were individuals to whom one went to get things done. I'm not trying to romanticise this lifestyle here, rather I'm trying to get across my memories of how the community operated.

When the incidents of homophobia & violence against women started to come through the grapevine, we were worried, naturally anxious, but did not initially have a focus for action. Then matters were brought to a head by an incident at the *Royal Park* pub; a man verbally abused a single mother, and threw glass in her baby's face. This incident brought things to a head. Rage and frustration boiled over. I recall sitting in a friend's house, together with a lesbian friend with whom I'd been doing some magical work with, and all three of us deciding that we had to do something. But what?

As far as I can recall, we spent some hours discussing what we were going to do. It wasn't a spur-of-the-moment action, but neither did anyone present that we wait until the morning, go off and consult someone else, or that we shouldn't act. Rather, the consensus was that we felt driven to act. We couldn't let this go on.

The ritual took place in the cellar of H., a woman who, though not into magic at the time was nonetheless sympathetic to it, together with her boyfriend of the time, C. The celebrants consisted of myself, and my lesbian friend, T.

Rather than target individuals, we decided to treat the behaviour—the male aggression against women and queers as a virus, or perhaps, a demon. However, we also felt it necessary to direct the Furies at M., the man involved in the glass-kicking incident which brought matters to a head. In using M. as the 'focus' for the Furies' attentions, it was intended that they would use him as a sample of the meme along the lines of: 'we want you to repel meme X, you can find an example of it in this particular host.'

I'm not going to go into the specifics of the ritual. Suffice to say that a variety of powers we felt appropriate were invoked, followed by a goetic spirit and its accompanying host.

As you might imagine, the atmosphere of the ritual space was charged with anticipation even before we began. As we began the preliminary invocations, we both noted a rise in temperature, and a feeling of electrical tension, a kind of pre-storm build-up which H. and her partner, who were in the sitting room above us, also perceived this. T. reported that during the Kali invocation, she felt herself to be tall, blue, with long, sharp fingernails, and felt a raw anger, almost psychopathic in intensity, building up —she felt, she said, a strong urge to rip me apart with her bare hands. She also 'heard' the sounds of clinking bracelets & ankle-bells).

T. then performed The Scream—visualising women of all races, in all cultures, in all eras, who have been oppressed, screaming their frustration and anger into the night (this is basically a visualisation sequence aimed at unleashing and focusing anger and determination). By this time we were both dripping with sweat and shaking. Upstairs, both H. & C. both reported a feeling of great activity below them, and a being 'pulled downwards' sensation. Apparently their two cats also reacted, going to them for comfort with their fur up and their eyes wide open.

At one point in the proceedings, H., on her way upstairs, saw what she later described as 'gneeches' - small, black, spindly-legged spirits flitting about. One appeared in front of her and she said something on the lines of 'Get back f**king down there' whereupon it made a chittering noise and vanished. She also observed that down in the sitting room, the temperature dropped and the room suddenly became windy (sudden winds blowing up had occurred during previous goetic operations).

T. reported later that she 'saw' Haures (the goetic spirit we had evoked) as an caucasian, blonde angel with a flowing gown, blood-red eyes, and a depraved smile. We both initially perceived him to appear in the Northern quadrant of the room, to which he returned until forcefully constrained. T said that she felt that the cellar was packed with spirits crowding around the circle. H., (upstairs) reported hearing feet stamping from below, and all present, to varying degrees, 'heard' an insect-like chittering noise. T. said she could smell horse-sweat, and perceived a strong sense of the 'nervous energy of horses'.

Pan Controlled Zone by Layla and Phil Legard - badges are available!

As Haures and the accompanying host were given their instructions, I felt them blast out of the cellar as a cloudy mass out of which dangled tangles of spindly legs. T. likened them to a plague of locusts, with the faces of angry women.

It is always difficult to gauge the success of a rite objectively. Over the weeks that followed, the local incidents of women or queer folk being harassed seemed (to us) to diminish. We also heard some reports of women who'd been abused by their male partners turning on them or leaving them. Shortly after the ritual, T., who at the time worked for Leeds City Council, was subjected to homophobic abuse by a male colleague, and her reaction was to punch him through a plate glass window! A work tribunal later concluded that she had been provoked and so she was not penalised.

The ritual also had personal effects on all involved. H. and her partner split up shortly afterwards, although how far this can be said to be a direct consequence of the rite is debatable. I suffered what amounted to a mini-nervous breakdown, which in retrospect, probably did me a lot of good.

Protest as Spectacle

The last kind of activism I want to discuss is activism that doesn't look like activism at all; it is the playful protest of street theatre, Discordian silliness; 'quiet' actions that are not obvious or non-threatening to the authorities. The attempts to levitate buildings fall into this category, inspired no doubt by the attempt to levitate the Pentagon in the 1960s.

On 21 October 1967, over 100,000 protesters gathered in front of the Pentagon to protest the Vietnam War. Several activists decided that a magical exorcism of the building was necessary—among them, the artist Michael Bowen, poet Gary Snyder and activist Jerry Rubin, later co-founder of the Youth International Party (Yippies). Bowen suggested that the ritual could levitate the building and drive from it all evil forces, bringing the Vietnam war to an abrupt end. Although some activists viewed the idea as merely symbolic, it seems that Bowen at least, took it very seriously.

The exorcism and the March was announced in the Underground Press of the period. During the ritual itself, Allen Ginsberg chanted mantras for its success; Abbie Hoffman encouraged couples to surround the Pentagon with public displays of affection, beaming love at it. Ed Sanders of the band The Fugs, performed what he later described as a 'Hittite exorcism'.

A recent example of such playful activism is Layla and Phil Legard's 'Pan Controlled Zone stickers' (see p49 for availability). The Pan Controlled Zone stickers were their response to the use of the kind of Zone Stickers and flyers that right-wing groups such as the British Freedom Party or National Action use to declare ownership of an area. Such stickers are one of the main mediums through which groups propagate their ideologies whilst maintaining anonymity and they have rapidly become a popular element of political expression. Layla and Phil write:

> The proscriptive nature of the zoning stickers and posters seemed ripe for some form of *détournement*, leading us to ask: what if we claimed a zone as a vision for some sort of idealised anarcho-paganism? What if we replaced 'do nots' with suggestions of things to do? How would we like to see people use their environments?

We should never underestimate the power of playfulness and offering positive possibilities. Also, I hear that magical activists have started to use the Pan stickers, and others like them, as 'wards' on buildings and around local public sites, not just of a protective nature, but also as means of marking them out as free enclaves; spaces of play and possibility.

A Space for Wonder

It can be difficult to maintain a sense of optimism when all about us seems dark and despondent. Yet an important element of magical activism that sometimes gets overlooked is the importance of daring to dream; to look beyond the bleak horizon and imagine what kind of life we want to build for ourselves and our allies. In order to do that we need space to dream; to wonder. As José Esteban Muñoz writes in *Cruising Utopia:*

> Astonishment helps one surpass the limitations of an alienating presentness and allows one to see a different time and place.

Wonder reorients us to that 'alienating presentness'—if only momentarily. Wonder is queer because it resists a monolithic signification; it's excessive, open, a recognition and embrace of difference.

Wonder is, in many ways, antithetical to utilitarian purposiveness, to the urge to categorise, to order. Wonder propels us towards the unfamiliar, to seek new relations, to revel in dizzying complexity and richness. Wonder pulls us into the world beyond a limited horizon, beyond the certain, the familiar, the possible. Wonder is excessive—and its excessive quality is something that western philosophy, trailing in the wake of Aristotle, has fought to foreclose, to rein in.

What would it be like to root ourselves in Wonder? We might allow that there is always space to be surprised, for doubt, for puzzles, for new feelings and experiences. We may consider ourselves as beings of wonder; not wholly knowable. And others too are wonders: not mysteries to be solved, dissected, analysed, but never known completely. We might suspend judgement, the fall into opposites. We might hesitate, allowing for the possibility of a dialogue, new discoveries. The capacity for wonder allows for possibilities as yet unimagined.

I reflect on the everyday experience that life is lived at different speeds (and times) and increasingly, it seems, the emphasis is on times/speeds being productive of something. Going places, moving through space, progressing towards goals, aims, tasks, achievements, with all the attendant self-monitoring and self-policing. The language, the speeds, the (regulatory) time of work has colonised every sphere of activity. Magic, and all its attendant extra-daily practices and attainments, has become work. At the same time, less present and less theorised, there are the gaps: the intermissions, spaces, the distractions; the pauses between and within purposeful activities and trajectories, in which a different magic may emerge.

There is more though, to be rooted in wonder as one's baseline orientation to the world is to experience ourselves as wonders. Think how disciplinary regimes: religion, spirituality, self-development, consumption all to varying degrees send the message that we are broken, cut off, in need of something to fill a void, not good enough. To be rooted in wonder can, I believe, help damp down those imperatives.

It is my contention that experiencing moments of wonder shifts us into a different world-space, forming new habits of experience and orientation. Habits are practices which tend to get routinely denigrated in many contemporary approaches to magical development, often because they are seen as things that need to be removed or conquered, or are seen as being imposed externally, as in the concept of social conditioning that individuals must ideally seek to disentangle themselves from. I'd suggest that it may be more productive to move past such negative perspectives on habits, and rather, to come at them as embodied practices.

How do we open ourselves to wonder? It may be as simple as going for a walk. Stopping for a break, chilling out, feeding the ducks. It is not about chasing down wonder, but allowing it to creep in when we least expect it. A first step might just be to slow down; allow yourself to see the world differently, if only for a moment.

Lingerings: a non-practice

Lingerings can be thought of as nonproductive micro-practices, momentary intensifications, sought and found within the gaps and pauses of purposive activity.

I let my eyes wander around me, alighting and resting in the shadow between keyboard and desk; on the shimmer of a peeling sticker on the side of the Dell box on my desk, on the stick figure frozen in the act of running on the fire exit sign over to my right. I let my hand caress an iron railing as I walk down some steps on the Thames embankment. Reading on screen, I idly caress the computer, the vibrations of its drives thrills throughout me. Pausing for a moment on the way to get my lunch, I'm momentarily enthralled by the way ripples dance across a pavement puddle. Such moments are small instances of finding/remembering the sense of immanent presence, the feeling of alive-ness.

Lingering also suggests the hauntings and traces of other moments on us; in memories, shared histories and affects; there at the edge of conscious awareness, the felt ghost-presences, at once familiar and strange; the co-minglings of thresholds that continually whirl around us, that we are immersed in. Through moments of wonder we may rediscover that the world is enchanted.

Enchantment is not some abstract quality, but blossoms in the joining together of hands, when many voices are raised in common purpose. To be enchanted is to discover delight and wonder. To discover that the world is full, that subjectivity is everywhere; blurring the boundaries between human/unhuman, matter/spirit, animate/inanimate. Moreover, enchantment is wild; we may open ourselves to it, but not command it. It is sensuous, and in the words of Val Plumwood, 'full of form, spirit, story, agency and glory'.

The motto of Hookland remains: **Re-Enchantment Is Resistance**.

Inspiring histories

When we stray beyond the parochial views of 20th-century British occultists it becomes obvious that magic for political means has been, and continues to be, deployed throughout the rest of the world. Here is a selection of examples from other cultures and the UK's history that give the lie to the notion that magic and politics are entirely separate domains and the two should never be mixed. Again, this is a personal selection, but we can take inspiration from the passion and activities of these occult 'ancestors'!

Political Astrology

In seventeenth-century England, astrology was very much a political tool, used to assess the qualities and flaws of political leaders. Also, it was illegal to use astrology to try and calculate the life expectancy of living monarchs, as this was considered to be close to performing a malevolent conjuration against a monarch. There were cases of astrologers being arrested for this crime. During the English Civil War, both Parliamentarians and Royalists used astrological assessments as a political tool. Al Cummins discusses the Early Modern political use of astrology in his 2012 book *The Starry Rubric: Seventeenth-Century English Astrology and Magic*, published by Hadean Press.

A Radical Spiritualist

The first English translation of Karl Marx's Communist Manifesto appeared in the American Spiritualist Newspaper, *Woodhull & Clafin's Weekly* in December 1871. This was Victoria Woodhull (1838-1927), suffragette, spiritualist, and free love advocate—although she later repudiated the latter. She was (arguably) the first woman to make a run for the American presidency, in 1872. Woodhull fell foul of the notorious Anthony Comstock after she published the details of an adulterous affair. She was charged, together with her husband and sister, with publishing an obscene newspaper and gross libel. Woodhull was still incarcerated when election day came along. The Woodhulls were later acquitted on a technicality. For more, see Barbara Goldsmith's entertaining book *Other Powers: The Age of Suffrage, Spiritualism, and the Scandalous Victoria Woodhull*.

"Red" Annie Besant

The Theosophical Society is not an esoteric movement much associated with either practical magic or political activism. However, we should acknowledge Annie Besant (1847-1933). Prior to her joining the Theosophical Society (in 1899) she had the reputation for being a political firebrand. Her first public lecture (1874) was entitled 'On the Political Status of Women' and she argued fiercely for the emancipation of women. Shortly afterwards, she joined Charles Bradlaugh's National Secular Society and co-edited its journal, *The National Reformer*. A successful and popular lecturer, Besant spoke out for women's rights, Irish home rule, family planning and trade unionism.

In 1877 she and Bradlaugh were put on trial for distributing a pamphlet on birth control. They were acquitted due to a technicality. Besant joined the socialist Fabian Society in 1885, and was also involved with the Social Democratic Federation. She worked together with the journalist W.T. Stead in campaigns against the exploitation of female and child labour, and furthering the cause of the trade union movement. Together they founded a weekly paper, *The Link*. In June 1888 she wrote an editorial entitled 'White Slavery in London' revealing the appalling working conditions and low wages of 'match-girls' employed at a factory in East London. The match-girls were paid low wages and were often fined if they arrived late for work or went to the toilet (sounds familiar!). Worse, fumes from the chemicals used in the manufacture of matches caused 'phossy jaw'—a form of bone cancer. In the wake of Besant's article, the factory owners sacked the women they thought had spoken to Besant. She, in her turn, helped the workers to form a trade union, and soon afterwards, the match-girls went on strike. The company gave in to their demands on July 21, re-instating the women who had been sacked and ending the system of fines. This was the first time that an unskilled workforce in London had successfully taken on factory bosses and won out.

On her initiation into the Theosophical Society, Besant recanted many of her earlier views and resigned as editor of *The National Reformer*. She first visited India in 1893 and settled there permanently in 1898. Annie Besant's involvement in Indian politics is complex, and I am not going to go into the details here. It's important to note however, that she founded the All India Home Rule League in 1916, which agitated for Independence through meetings and protests. Between June and September 1917 Besant was interned on the orders of the Viceroy of India, Lord Chelmsford, a move that occasioned protests across India. In December 1917 she was elected to the post of president of the Indian National Congress. She continued to speak out for women's rights in India and Home Rule for the rest of her life.

Anna Kingsford and Animal Rights

Anna Bonus Kingsford (1846–1888), in addition to her occult practice, journalism and novels, was a fervent campaigner for women's rights and an anti-vivisectionist. She was one of the first women in England to qualify as a medical doctor. According to Kingsford's former magical partner Edward Maitland, Kingsford attempted to carry out a magical attack against Louis Pasteur, as she was opposed to his experiments with animals. A description of the incident can be found in Maitland's *Anna Kingsford: Her Life, Letters, Diary, and Work* (1896) published after her death. Maitland burned all of Kingsford's papers after publishing his book so there is no way of substantiating this story.

Florence Farr

Florence Farr is mostly remembered by occultists for her leading role in the Hermetic Order of the Golden Dawn, but she was also an avid supporter of women's rights and suffrage. In 1910, she published *Modern Women: Her Intentions*—a collection of essays in which she argued for women's suffrage, rights to education, inclusion in the professions, and reform of the divorce laws. In one essay, 'The Rights of Astaroth' (also published in *The New Age*) she made the case that not only should prostitution be legalized, but that it should be made a sacred office, as it was in ancient Egypt.

On February 2, 1911, Huntley Carter, editor of *The New Age*, published *A Women's Suffrage Supplement*, featuring opinions on Women's Suffrage from a variety of well-known figures.

Florence Farr made the following points:

1. "Fools, not women, should be voteless.
2. No man can be expected to give the vote to anyone who visibly wants to keep him in order with it.
3. The vote will have to be taken by force, not given; that is what makes it worth having.
4. I should get rid of women's delusions about young girls and their education. The young could win the battle in a week if they would only try."

A lesson from India: Kali against the British

In the nineteenth and twentieth centuries, the goddess Kali was frequently invoked to fuel anti-colonial fervour in India. Bankimchandra

Chattopadhyay's 1882 novel *Anandamath*—set during the 1770 famine, compares India under foreign rule to the domain of Kali, the land become a cremation ground; and looks forwards to a time in the future when the power of the Mother stretches in all the ten directions. Activists such as Bipin Chandra Pal circulated pamphlets suggesting that Kali pujas should be enacted in every village and that Kali would rouse the energies of the nation—that just as Kali defeated the asuras who had usurped the rule of the gods, so would Bengal drive out the British. It was also suggested that the goddess should be given 108 white goats as a sacrifice: 'sacrificing a white goat to Kali' being a euphemism for killing an Englishman. Across India, voices were raised supplicating Kali to begin her dance of destruction and trample down the demonic British.

In 1907 a lithographic print of Kali (advertising a local brand of cigarettes) was produced by the Calcutta Art Studio. Herbert H. Risley, a colonial administrator, deemed it seditious, believing that the garland of heads Kali was adorned with were European and that a decapitated head in the right lower corner of the image was that of a British soldier. The Times correspondent Sir Valentine Chirol, in his 1910 book *Indian Unrest*, made much of the close relationship between Indian unrest and 'the cult of the terrible goddess' and 'the horrible and obscene rites of Shakti worship'; quoting a Bengali publication 'What have we learned from the Shakti Puja? Sooner or later this great Puja will yield the desired results. When the Hindus realize the true magnificence of the Mother, they will be roused from the slumber of ages, and the auspicious dawn of awakenment will light up the horizon.'

A Bengali newspaper, *Jugantar*, founded in 1906 by Barindra Kumar Ghosh and Abhinash Bhattacharya, openly advocated for the overthrow of British rule and featured essays aimed at mobilizing popular support for revolution. Its editor, Bhupendranath Dutt, was arrested and charged with sedition in 1907 and closed down by the authorities in 1908. *Jugantar's* activists frequently called upon the goddess in her ferocious forms—Kali, Durga, Kalika, representing her as thirsting for blood; a thirst that could only be quenched by the blood of the invaders.

New Pagans: the Kindred of the Kibbo Kift

The Kindred of the Kibbo Kift was founded in 1920 by John Hargrave. 'Kibbo Kift' is a colloquial term from the county of Cheshire, meaning 'proof of strength'. Hargrave had originally been a leader in the Boy Scouts, but he fell out with Baden-Powell, for he had strong anti-militaristic and anti-imperialist views, and Baden-Powell 'excommunicated' Hargreaves from the Scouts movement.

The Kibbo Kift was much more than one of the woodcraft movements that sprang up following the first World War. Hargreaves had a strong interest in paganism, the occult, and the group's camp activities were often opened with a ritual 'beating of the bounds'. As early as 1919, Hargrave had written about the benefits of yoga and meditation. Members were encouraged to adopt kith names (Hargreaves' name was 'White Fox') and create their own personal symbols. The Kindred are known to have made frequent visits to sites such as Silbury Hill, Avebury, Stonehenge and the Cerne Abbas Giant. On one occasion in 1929, they arrived at Stonehenge only to find it already occupied by Druids. Hargrave encouraged members of the Kindred to study comparative religion, and drew inspiration from both Theosophy and the writings of Aleister Crowley.

The Kindred was not celebrating England's ancient past, but looked towards the future. Hargrave believed that the Kindred should inspire people to adopt the values of not only serving one's own community, but also the world at large. In 1924 Hargrave proclaimed a new, utopian vision for the future based on the Social Credit system first devised by C.H. Douglas. Hargrave believed that 'enjoyment' not employment, was the key to life, and argued that all persons should receive a state-paid benefit, and that the necessity of work in order to live a decent life would become unnecessary.

Hargrave formally disbanded the Kibbo Kift in 1931, but what emerged was the Green Shirt Movement for Social Credit. The Green Shirts marched, distributed leaflets and organized protests against the banking system. In 1934, a green-painted brick was hurled through the window of 11 Downing Street. In 1937, the Green Shirts were outlawed under the terms of the Public Order Act that banned quasi-military political movements. It was aimed at groups such as Oswald Moseley's Black Shirts. The Green Shirts' gesture of greeting—an open palm raised in greeting, was identified with the Hitler Salute in the public eye, and of course the initials of the Kindred, K.K.K also helped foster the idea that the group was allied with the far right.

If you want to know more about the Kindred of the Kibbo Kift, I'd recommend Annebella Pollen's *The Kindred of the Kibbo Kift: Intellectual Barbarians* (Donlon Books).

Points to Consider

- Be Passionate!
- Be Inclusive!
- Make Alliances.
- Give Options. If you're planning a ritual, allow people to choose how they want to participate.
- Plan Ahead. Multiple or flexible plans are much more effective than expecting that a single plan will survive contact with reality. Things that sound fine in a discussion or on paper may not work out exactly as you envision them.
- Small Steps can be productive. Small actions gather momentum and enthusiasm for larger events.
- Think before you act. What is the best way to intervene or help in a particular situation? Ask advice.
- Rotate Roles. If one person has the same job to do they are more likely to burn out or get bored. Rotating jobs is an excellent way of sharing skills and expertise.
- Know your enemy.
- Know the Law.
- Learn to work the media.
- Consider Non-Violent Direct Action.
- What are the ethical implications?

Further Reading and Resources

Links

Dragon Ecomagick

http://www.dragonnetwork.org/index.htm

Both of the ebooks I mentioned can be downloaded from this page.

http://www.dragonnetwork.org/tools.htm

Accounts of Stop the City

https://history-is-made-at-night.blogspot.com/2011/10/stop-city-1984.html

https://dangerousminds.net/comments/the_original_occupy_wall_street_stop_the_city_1984

Fracking

https://wildhunt.org/2016/12/calling-all-warriors-pagans-in-the-uk-anti-fracking-campaigns.html

https://www.cpre.org.uk/explainer/what-is-fracking/

The Black Djinn Curse:

http://www.chaosmatrix.org/library/chaos/texts/apikbdc.html

Layla and Phil Legard's essay, *Materia Magica Nova: Towards a Critical Magic:*

https://larkfall.wordpress.com/2020/03/12/materia-magica-nova-towards-a-critical-magic/

Christine Ferguson's excellent essay: *Anna Kingsford and the Intuitive Science of Occultism*

https://brill.com/view/journals/arie/22/1/article-p114_6.xml

Abram J Lewis. 2015. *The Falling Dream: Unreason and Enchantment in the Gay Liberation Movement*. Ph.D thesis, University of Minnesota. PDF

https://conservancy.umn.edu/bitstream/handle/11299/190541/Lewis_umn_0130E_16266.pdf?sequence=1

Books

Owen Davies. 2018. *A Supernatural War: Magic, Divination, and Faith during the First World War*. Oxford University Press. A fantastic book exploring the use of magical practices on the home front and the battlefield during World War I.

Joy Dixon. 2001. *Divine Feminine: Theosophy and Feminism in England*. The John Hopkins University Press. An excellent study of the Theosophical Society and radical politics.

Shai Feraro. 2016. 'Invoking Hecate at the Women's Peace Camp: The Presence of Goddess Spirituality and Dianic Witchcraft at Greenham Common in the 1980s'. *Magic, Ritual, and Witchcraft*. Winter 2016, Volume II.2

Shai Feraro. 2020. *Women and Gender Issues in British Paganism, 1945-1990*. Palgrave Macmillan. Shai Feraro has done some thorough research into the expressions and tensions between feminist activisms and various strands of the UK's esoteric subcultures.

Barbara Goldsmith. 1998. *Other Powers: The Age of Suffrage, Spiritualism, and the Scandalous Victoria Woodhull*. Alfred A. Knopf. Good book on Woodhull and her doings.

George McKay (ed), 1998. *DiY Culture: Party and Protest in 90s Britain*.Verso. Nothing occult here, but there's some good essays in this collection about the road protest movement, the 'reclaim the streets' activism of the later 1990s, and how worship of the land can all too easily tip into nationalist excesses.

Patricia MacCormack. 2020. *The Ahuman Manifesto: Activism for the End of the Anthropocene*. Bloomsbury. A radical call for new forms of activism and modes of becoming to move towards a different world with passion and grace.

José Esteban Muñoz. 2019. *Cruising Utopia: The Then and There of Queer Futurity (10th Anniversary Edition)*. New York University Press. Argues that queerness is a future-oriented, utopian approach to being and doing. Inspirational.

Kirsty Ryder. 2022. *Radical Witchcraft: Oppression and Resistance*. The Museum of Witchcraft and Magic. A small book exploring the tangled history of magical resistance to oppression. Lots of pictures and a very thorough bibliography.

Starhawk. 1982. *Dreaming the Dark: Magic, Sex and Politics*. Beacon Press. In terms of magical activism, this is the book that "radicalized" me. It was a wake-up call.

Zeynep Tufekci. 2017. *Twitter and Tear Gas: The Power and Fragility of Networked Protest*. Yale University Press. A critical but not unsympathetic look at the role of social media in protest movements.

Francis Young. 2022. *Magic in Merlin's Realm: A History of Occult Politics in Britain*. Cambridge University Press. I've only just acquired a copy of this book, but it does look very comprehensive, exploring the intersection between occultism and politics throughout British history.

Supporter websites and books

This small book would not have been possible without the kind support of those who gave me permission to reproduce their artwork or quote freely from their books. If you have enjoyed this book, please consider supporting those who made it possible.

Al Cummins

Al Cummins' books are available from Hadean Press

https://www.hadeanpress.com/shop

Lawrence Burton

A selection of Lawrence Burton's published books can be purchased fom Lulu:

https://www.lulu.com/spotlight/12flower

Layla and Phil Legard

Follow Layla and Phil Legards' musical (Hawthonn) and writing productions here:

https://larkfall.wordpress.com/

The wonderful 'Pan-Controlled Zone' stickers (page 36) can be purchased here, along with other Hawthonn-related merchandise:

https://xetb.bandcamp.com/merch

Patricia MacCormack

Patricia MacCormack's most recent book is *The Ahuman Manifesto: Activism for the End of the Anthropocene*.

https://www.bloomsbury.com/uk/ahuman-manifesto-9781350081109/

David Southwell

Follow David Southwell's Hookland Guide on Substack.

https://substack.com/profile/108817871-hookland

Maria Strutz

Maria Strutz' online shop for limited edition prints.

https://maria-strutz.onlineweb.shop/

About the Author

Phil Hine has been a practising Occultist for over forty-five years, with a career spanning Wicca, Ritual Magic, Chaos Magic and nondual Tantra. Together with Rodney Orpheus he co-created and edited the UK's first monthly Pagan magazine, *Pagan News* (1988-92). He is a former initiate of the Illuminates of Thanateros, The Esoteric Order of Dagon, and the Arcane & Mystical Order of the Knights of Shamballa (AMOOKOS). He was an activist in Pagan networks in the 1980s such as PaganLink and HOBLink—the UK's first network for LGBTQ occult practitioners. He lives in London, England.

Personal blog:

https://enfolding.org/

Substack Newsletter:

https://philhine.substack.com/

Phil's books include: *Condensed Chaos*, *Prime Chaos*, *The Pseudonomicon*, and *Hine's Varieties: Chaos & Beyond*. His most recent work is *Queerying Occultures* (2023). All these titles are available from the Original Falcon Press.

https://originalfalcon.com/products.php?a=phil_hine

Twisted Trunk

Twisted Trunk was founded in 2019. In addition to this book, we have also published:

Yakṣiṇī Magic by Mike Magee (2019) and ***Kālī Magic*** by Mike Magee (2022)

Both of these books are available in print and digital editions via Amazon. For more information about these titles, visit

https://enfolding.org/books/

Printed in Great Britain
by Amazon

61872620R00033